APPL[illegible]

EDITION

The Answer to All Your Series 3 Questions

Table of Contents

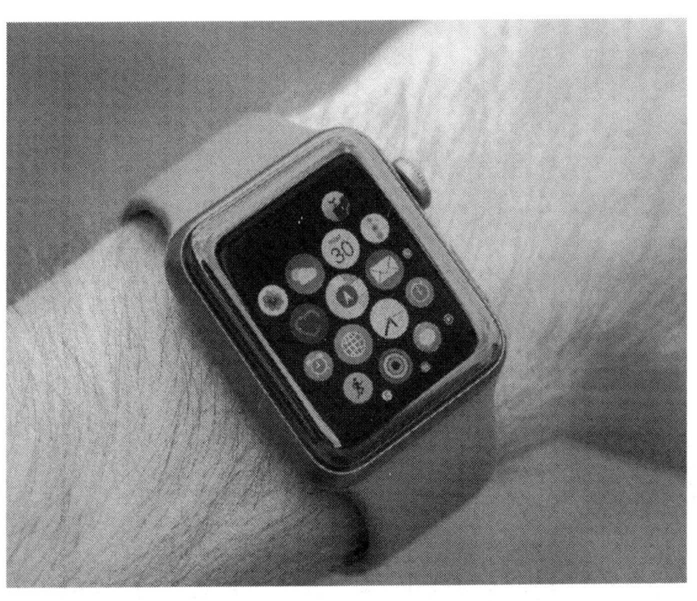

Introduction

With the vision of creating an all-inclusive, touchable, and wearable computing device, Apple debuted their Apple Watch, Apple's take on the ever more popular smartwatch, in the latter months of 2016. Aesthetically pleasing as most Apple products are, the Apple Watch, at the time, offered users a stylish and functional alternative to the traditional watch.

Not only could Apple's first timepiece tell, as you might imagine, time, it could also make and take calls, send and receive texts, track your workouts, operate most social media apps, and much more. However, the Apple Watch was merely a pretty accessory, redundant in terms of its functions. What could the watch do that the phone could not? Furthermore, the Apple Watch most notably lacked cellular connectivity, essentially hinging the functionality of the timepiece to its owner's iPhone.

In other words, if your iPhone runs out of battery, your Apple Watch Series 1 or 2, due to its lack of cellular connection, would not be able to receive calls, rendering the timepiece more of a cosmetic extension to the iPhone than an effective standalone device. Users needed to bring both their watch and iPhone with them to get any use out of the former. So, Apple went back to the drawing board, trying to design a smartwatch that would allow its users to leave the phone at home and bring just the timepiece.

Released in September 2017, the Apple Watch Series 3 marked Apple's fix to the problem of redundancy: add cellular connectivity to the newest Apple Watch, providing users with the option to leave their phones at home and simply wear the smartwatch out. So, what majorly differentiates the Apple Watch Series 3 from its predecessors is its LTE cellular connectivity, represented by the striking red digital crown on the right side of the watch face. Users do not need to carry their phones around because the Apple Watch Series 3 has its own functioning cellular connection. Also, with the S3 chip, an upgrade to the Series 3, the user will experience a much-improved responsiveness to the device in comparison to previous models. Thus, the Apple Watch Series 3 is an upgrade on its predecessors in both processing speed and its ability to standalone from the user's mobile device.

Having established the basic background information for the Apple Watch Series 3, this book will guide you on how to get the most out of your timepiece, whether it be aesthetically or functionally. The Apple Watch perfectly intersects style and utility, so why not optimize both? What will follow is three parts: a buyer's guide on assembling the watch that you want; a tutorial on how to operate the watch and its major apps; and how to personalize the functions of the watch.

PART I
Purchasing the Right Apple Watch Series 3 for You

When it comes to purchasing the right Apple Watch Series 3, the ostensibly limitless customization options can cause much hesitation and doubt. What band should I buy? What color case should I buy? How much will it all cost? There's no need to stress and research your options for hours—just peruse the comprehensive overview of the choices available to you below.

1. General Specifications (from Apple website)

Series 3 (GPS) Features

- Built-in GPS and GLONASS
- Faster dual-core processor
- W2 chip
- Barometric altimeter
- Capacity 8GB
- Heart rate sensor
- Accelerometer and gyroscope
- Water resistant 50 meters

- Ion-X strengthened glass
- Composite back
- Wi-Fi (802.11b/g/n 2.4GHz)
- Bluetooth 4.2
- Up to 18 hours of battery life3
- Watch OS 4

Series 3 (GPS + Cellular) Features

- Built-in GPS and GLONASS
- Faster dual-core processor
- W2 chip
- Barometric altimeter
- Capacity 16GB
- Heart rate sensor
- Accelerometer and gyroscope
- Water resistant 50 meters
- Ion-X strengthened glass
- Ceramic back
- Wi-Fi (802.11b/g/n 2.4GHz)

- Bluetooth 4.2
- Up to 18 hours of battery life
- Watch OS 4

A Few Definitions

The following are definitions for some of the terms listed above so that the layman can understand precisely what the Series 3 offers.

GLONASS - An acronym for Global Navigation Satellite System, GLONASS was developed in Russia. It was the Soviet Union's answer to the United States' widely known GPS. GLONASS alone does not provide the strength of coverage that GPS does; nevertheless, the Russian technology thrives in its accuracy and capacity to track you between skyscrapers and subways—two areas which GPS cannot cover. So, with the Series 3, you get a device that has both GLONASS and GPS, allowing for the great coverage wherever you are going.

W2 Chip - According to Apple, the W2 chip—an upgrade from the W1 chip—delivers boosted Wi-Fi speeds and makes the watch more power efficient when using Bluetooth and Wi-Fi in comparison to the previous generations of the Apple Watch. Ultimately, the W2 chip renders the Series 3 a more efficient device than the

Series 1 or 2, addressing possible battery life issues users might have.

Barometric Altimeter - New to the Apple Watch Series 3, the barometric altimeter allows the watch to track elevation in your workouts. The barometric altimeter basically assesses how altitude affects your body during your exercises.

Accelerometer and gyroscope - Both are sensors that track and record motion data. Getting reads on your sleep patterns, your heartrate, your breathing are all done by these sensors.

Ion-X Strengthened Glass - Apple's scratch-resistant technology used for their Apple Watch displays. This is their alternative to the traditional sapphire glass often used for regular watch faces.

2. LTE Cellular vs. Non-Cellular/GPS-only

As stated in the introduction, Apple differentiated the Apple Watch Series 3 from its predecessors by incorporating LTE cellular connectivity to the device. That being said, Apple does offer the Series 3 in a non-cellular option; however, going with this option brings back the redundancy issue. But, it is not only in cellular connectivity that these two options differ. The LTE Cellular Series 3 has 16GB of storage to the Non-cellular's 8GB; the LTE Cellular Series 3 offers many more casing options while the Non-Cellular is restricted to aluminum casings; the battery life averages about 18 hours of use for both. Nevertheless, if you are an individual who likes to have their phone always on hand, then, perhaps, the non-cellular Series 3 would be the best choice for you.

After deciding on whether you want cellular connectivity or not, you simply need to choose what watch size you want. Both the Cellular and Non-cellular versions come in 38mm and 42mm. The thing to take into account here is, if you want a Hermes watch single or double tour watch band, each only fits on one size.

3. Casing Options

For the GPS-only version of the Series 3, the casing options are quite limited—in actuality, aluminum is the only available casing material for the Non-cellular watch. Given that, you do get to choose the color of the casing, but even that choice is restricted to silver, gold, and space gray (a dark grey verging on black). GPS-only Series 3 watches go for $329.

The Cellular Series 3 gives a few more options in regards to casing material:

For the buyer looking for the cheapest option, Apple offers the Cellular Series 3 in the aluminum casings that are used for the GPS-only Series 3. These casings come in the same colors as the Non-cellular casings. The Cellular Series 3 goes for $399 in the aluminum casing, $70 more than the GPS-only version.

The second option, the mid-price casing material, is stainless steel. This casing material comes in a glossy, metallic silver color or space grey. The stainless steel casing proves much more resilient than the aluminum casing, providing a "diamond-like carbon" (DLC) coating. This casing material is the most reminiscent of traditional timepieces, with its classic and abiding style and strength.

The 'high-end' option is the ceramic casing option. While the ceramic casing is even harder than steel, it is also more prone to shattering on a hard surface than the stainless-steel casing is. In essence, the ceramic casing is the most scratch-resistant out of the three options, but it is not as robust a material as stainless steel. The casing comes in two simple color options: white or black. Ceramic Series 3 models begin at $1299, quite a significant increase in price from the stainless steel option.

4. Band Options

Again, just like with the casing options for the Series 3 GPS-only watch, the band options are quite limited. The first option is the sport band, which comes in the colors fog (a light grey color), pink sand (a cream pink color), space gray, and black. The sport band is composed of fluoroelastomer, a synthetic rubber that resists most chemicals. The second options is the Nike + sport band, which is composed of fluoroelastomer as well, but comes in the pure platinum (white) and the anthracite colors. The difference between the two bands is purely cosmetic, both priced at the same value. The normal sport band is quite plain while the Nike + sport band comes covered with little holes, allowing for breathability.

The band options for the Series 3 Cellular do not leave much to be desired. However, depending on the casing you purchase, your band options may be more or less limited, still. If desired, you can purchase the normal sport band or Nike + sport band with all three casings. The Series 3 Cellular does have alternative cheap options: the sport loop and the Nike + sport loop. The sport loop is made of a nylon material and comes in black, seashell (a silver color), and pink sand. The Nike + sport loop comes in midnight fog (a grey green color) and black/platinum. The only difference between the normal sport loop and the Nike + sport loop is the available colors. So, for the aluminum version of the Series 3 Cellular, the sport bands and sport loops are your options.

The stainless steel casing has the most band options available. As stated before, the sport bands and loops can be purchased with the stainless steel casing, but for those looking for more expensive bands, the Milanese loop is another option. The Milanese loop, a stainless steel mesh developed in Italy, allows for the user to find a personalized fit for their watch because of its magnetic properties. In other words, the Milanese loop is infinitely adjustable. Series 3 watches that come with the Milanese loop start at $699. If you want the watch with the space grey Milanese loop, then the price increases to $749. Furthermore, the stainless steel casing has the Hermes—the French luxury goods manufacturer—collaboration option. The Hermes bands offer a leather alternative, bringing a classic, traditional look to Apple's smartwatch. The single tour option, for the most part, can only be paired with the 42mm size casing; the double tour option with the 38mm size casing. There are a few exceptions to the single tour band, allowing it to be compatible with both casing sizes. The two main colors for the Hermes bands are fauve and indigo, and the stainless steel Series 3 with the Hermes band starts at $1299.

The options for the ceramic casing are even more limited than the band options for the aluminum casing. Nevertheless, the sport band that comes with the ceramic casing comes with ceramic accents while the aluminum sport band only has aluminum accents. The color options are black and white.

Note: Only the sport band and sport loop are water-resistant. So, these bands would be best for those who want to exercise while wearing the Series 3.

What should be known is that third-party companies have designed their own bands. The information provided above covers the factory options Apple offers on its website. If none of the options sound particularly appealing to you, the bands, out of all the physical components of the Series 3, is the easiest to customize. A search on the internet will bring up a profusion of alternative options not offered by Apple. Undoubtedly, most people will be able to find some band design they like, even if it is not sold by a company other than Apple.

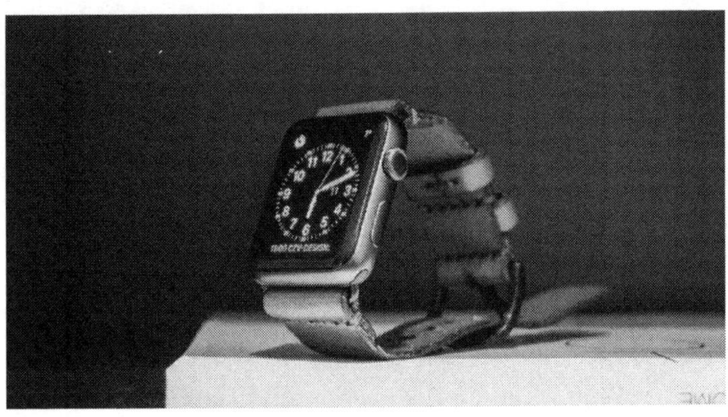

Simplifying the Choice

To simplify your choice, this is a distillation of the information covered in this section:

- Decide whether you want cellular connectivity or not. Granted, LTE Cellular is the main innovation of the Apple Watch Series 3, but if you do not mind the watch's functionality being tethered to your iPhone, then there is no need to pay the upcharge. Furthermore, you should know that, to even use cellular on your watch, you need to sign up for a plan with a provider such as AT&T. This will, of course, incur a monthly cost of ~$10.

- Take into consideration that Cellular vs. Non-Cellular is not the only differentiating factor between the two versions of the Series 3. The Series 3 Cellular comes with double the storage, a plethora of stock band options, and a ceramic back. The Series 3 GPS-only comes with a composite back, making the underside of the watch more prone to scratching and breakage in comparison to the Series 3 Cellular's back.

- Aluminum casings, while the cheapest option, are not particularly resilient. Scratches will easily show on your casing. Also, the aluminum casing does not come with as many band options as the stainless steel casing does. That being said, the aluminum casing is also the lightest material out of the three casing variations. This casing could be best for athletes or those living an active lifestyle as it is lightweight but also the most affordable to replace out of the three casings. You will not feel weighed down or have to constantly worry about damaging one of the more expensive casings if you go for the aluminum option. The aluminum Series 3 is also the best entry point for those who want to try out Apple's timepiece without having to break the bank, per say. Series 3 GPS-only costs $329; Series 3 Cellular prices costs $399.

- Stainless steel casings and the mid-range option in price, is resilient but not as scratchproof as the ceramic casing. If you have no interest in buying a band from a third-party seller, then the stainless steel Series 3 has the most stock band options available, ranging from the sport band to the supple leather Hermes bands. The stainless steel casing also delivers a classic look as it is a material often used for traditional, luxury time-pieces. Thus, the stainless steel Series 3 fuses timeless style and modern technology that want a sophisticated workhorse. You will not have the worry about breakage with the stainless steel casing whatsoever. Stainless steel Series 3 prices start at $599 and can, when packaged with one of the Hermes bands, go for up to $1299.

- Ceramic casings, the unique but pricey option, will distinguish you from everyone else in the sea of Apple Watch wearers, but only for the price of $1299. The band options are the most limited out of all the three's, but the ceramic casing, while not as resilient as the stainless steel casing, is the most scratch-resistant.
- Keep in mind, as well, that the limited stock band options for each casing should be the least of your concerns. You can always search for one that is offered by a third-party seller and switch it out with the one that comes packaged with your Series 3.

PART II
Using Your Apple Watch Series 3

Controlling the Apple Watch

As far as interacting or physically operating the Apple Watch Series 3 goes, the controls are quite simple. Looking at the picture above, you see the three main components that the user needs to utilize their watch: the watch face, the dial/digital crown, and the side button.

1. The Watch Face

Akin to most smart devices, the watch face is operated by touch. To make full use of the Series 3, the user must familiarize themselves with four gestures/actions.

1. Tap—action used to select buttons on the display and "wake up" the display.
2. Press or "Force touch"—action that allows user to go to options in apps and change the look of their watch face.
3. Drag—action that involves keeping the finger on the display and scrolling or adjusting sliders. For example, the drag gesture is used to navigate the Maps app because you may need to adjust what part of the map you want to look at on the screen.
4. Swipe—action that can be performed in all four directions (up, down, left, and right) and involves a quick swipe of the finger on the display.

2. The Dial/Digital Crown

Again, the red coloration of this component clearly differentiates the Series 3 Cellular and the GPS-only versions. Nevertheless, the digital crown functions the same way for both. Two actions can be performed using the digital crown: press and rotate. The press gesture can, depending on the number and length of presses, result in different commands.

1. Short press—returns the user to the home screen, which can be the user's personalized watch screen.

2. Press and hold—triggers Siri, Apple's AI that can perform basic tasks such as a Google search for the user.

3. Double-click/double-press—returns the user to the last used application.

4. Rotate—rotating the digital crown can zoom, scroll, or adjust what it is on the screen.

5. Slow rotation when watch screen is off—this action will gradually increase or decrease the brightness of the display.

3. The Side Button

The side button—the oval shaped button under the digital crown—is the third component necessary for operating your Apple Watch Series 3. As you might expect, the user must press the side button for it to work, but depending on the number and length of presses, different commands will be triggered.

1. Short press—shows or hides the Dock (a scrolling page of the user's favorite/most-used apps, more on this later).

2. Long press and hold—gives user the option to send out a SOS, but also just works to turn the device on and off.

3. Double-click/double-press—starts the Apple Pay application.

How to use the Main Applications/Features

The Apple Watch Series 3 - at least, the Cellular version - is meant to provide the same service and features as the iPhone does. Apple includes the essentials in the watch, allowing users to leave their phone at home.

1. Siri

Siri is Apple's "Intelligent Assistant," which will help you navigate your Apple Watch. You can activate her by pressing and holding the digital crown or saying "Hey, Siri." Siri offers the easiest way of getting to the exact app you want to use without having to use your hands.

2. Home Screen

The Home Screen is the "page," which displays all of the apps you have downloaded on your Apple Watch. To get to the Home Screen, you simply press the digital crown once. The total number of apps you have on the watch is completely up to you—or in some cases, depends on how much storage you have. There are two options available for the look of the Home Screen: honeycomb and list.

i. Honeycomb

Intended to loosely mimic the appearance of a honeycomb, this default option is aesthetically pleasing. However, the more apps you have, the more cluttered the Home Screen looks, making navigating the screen more difficult. Here, the rotation function on the digital crown comes in handy as you can zoom in and zoom out of the page, allowing you to see more or fewer apps depending on how close or far you have set the zoom.

If you would like to rearrange your apps, you force touch one of your apps, causing all of them to jiggle. You can now drag your apps around so that they are configured the way you want them to be. Force touching also allows you to remove an app from your watch completely. This will not delete the corresponding app on your iPhone, though.

ii. List

The more functional option of the two, the list view is as simple as it sounds. Your Home Screen will simply be a list of your apps. Considering the functionality of the Dock - more on this next - the Home Screen may not even be a feature that you frequently use. Nevertheless, the list may not be visually attractive, but it gets the job done.

> Tip: Rather than use the Home Screen, Siri seems to be the most effective and expedient option to navigating the Apple Watch Series 3. Just press and hold the digital crown to activate her.

3. The Dock

What is the Dock? Well, it is a list of your favorite applications. You can swipe or scroll through miniature "pages" or snapshots of your most-used apps. If you want to add an app to your dock, you start up whatever application it is and then press the side button. A button asking you whether you want to keep the app in the Dock will appear, and you just tap the button if you do. If you wish to remove an application from your Dock, you press the side button, scroll to the app, and swipe up. The option to remove the app from your Dock should appear as an X symbol. In essence, the Dock serves as the quickest method to get to the apps you use the most.

4. The Control Center

Just like the iPhone's Control Center, the Apple Watch Series 3 has its own simplified version. The Control Center gives you quick and easy access to the essential settings of the watch. To get to the Control Center, you simply swipe up from the main watch face screen, revealing the hidden page. The Control Center shows you how much battery life you have left, allows you to connect to your Bluetooth headphones, turn the watch into a flashlight, silence the watch, and turn on airplane mode. If you purchased the Cellular version, the Wi-Fi and Cellular Data buttons will also be found in the Control Center.

Tip: If you are using the Apple AirPods, checking the battery life of the watch will also show you the battery life of your AirPods. There is also the battery saver option if you check your battery life.

5. Making and Taking Calls

Probably one of, if not the most, important features of a phone is the ability to call—isn't that the point of a phone? Of course, for most modern consumers, the whole process of making and taking calls comes as second nature, so it should be pretty intuitive with the Apple Watch, as well.

When someone is calling you, the number appears on your display, giving you the option of accepting or rejecting the call with the tap gesture. If you swipe up, the Apple Watch gives you the option to reject with a text message or answer the call on your iPhone. The Series 3 does not have an audio jack, meaning you must have Bluetooth headphones/earbuds unless you are fine with your conversation being public. When in the call, the volume control appears as a slider at the top of the display. To adjust the volume you can just tap the + or – sign depending on your preferences.

Making calls is harder than taking one. The best way to make a phone call is to press and hold the digital crown in order to trigger Siri. You can just dictate the number or the name (if the individual is in your friends/contacts list) to her. Another method to phone people is to use the Phone app. Your Apple Watch should be synced to your iPhone, so all of your contacts should be present in the timepiece. You simply start the Phone app and scroll through your contacts—pretty self-explanatory.

6. Messages

Similarly to making a call, the easiest way to send a text would be through Siri. A command such as "Siri, I want to send a text to X" works. Otherwise, you can manually go to the Message app on the Series 3 through the Dock or the Home Screen. After selecting the chat or person you want to message, you have three options: dictation; emoji; and digital touch.

Dictation, as the denotation of the word suggests, is when you speak into your watch, and it will record and transcribe your message into text form. Remember that you need to say the punctuation you want in your sentence. For example, if you want to end your sentence with a period, you need to dictate "period."

The emoji message gives you the option to send any kind of emoji from Apple's extensive catalogue to your recipient. Perhaps, the most interesting messaging option is the Series 3's digital touch feature.

Digital touch allows the you to send an image sketched on the screen, taps, kisses (tap two fingers on screen one or more times), your heartbeat (place two fingers on screen until you feel your heartbeat and see a visual of a heart), a broken heart (swipe down after copying the process to get your heartbeat, and anger (touch and hold one finger on the screen). You can change the colors of all these visuals by tapping the circle in the top right of the display.

Currently, the Apple Watch Series 3 does not have the capability to send images. You can, however, transfer your photos from your iPhone to your Apple Watch, so you can view your pictures on the timepiece. You can also receive photos from others through messages, as well.

7. Notifications

Notifications are the exact same as the ones you receive on your smartphone. They can range from text messages to tweets to news alerts. Just apply the same alert/ notification feed you have on your phone, and that is what you get on the Apple Watch. Notifications will go directly to your timepiece when your iPhone is locked.

When you receive a notification, swipe left to get the option to delete it, tap on it to get all of the text, and clear all by force touching. To regulate what notifications you want on your watch, you need to use the My Watch app on your iPhone and decide which apps you would like notifications from.

8. Maps and Directions

Just like with all the other applications, you can access the Maps app by activating Siri, finding it on your Home Screen, or going to your Dock, if you have added the Maps app to it. Also, the Maps app will start if you click on an address in a text or email.

After starting the Maps app, you need to tap the My Location button. This will take you to your location on the digital map. From here, you can rotate the digital crown to zoom in or zoom out from where you currently are. Alternatively, you can simply use the drag gesture to manually control what part of the map is on the display. To return to the main screen, hit the back arrow at the top left.

If you are looking for directions to a specific place or just nearby shopping, dining, gas, etc. locations, you can start the search from the main menu of the Maps app. After deciding on where you intend to go, the Apple Watch will give you the choice of walking, driving, or public transport directions. Twelve steady vibrations means that you will need to turn right; three pairs of two vibrations means that you will need to turn left. The Apple Watch alerts you that you are near your destination with vibrations, as well.

At the top left, you have the option to either see the estimated time of arrival or the amount of time left to get to your destination. You can toggle between the two by simply tapping the top left.

If you want to stop receiving directions, you need to force touch the screen. The Stop Directions button will pop up as a circle with an x in the middle. Perhaps, if you have a good idea of how to get to your destination, you should stop receiving directions in order to conserve your battery, especially when you have left your iPhone at home.

> Tip: If you tend to use a certain mode of transportation, you can set a default from the My Watch app on your iPhone

9. Viewing Reminders and the Calendar app

In order to use the Calendar app on the Series 3, you need to have it first set up on an iPhone. Your Calendar app can be synced with Google Calendar, Facebook, Exchange, Yahoo, and some other services. As with all other applications, there are multiple methods to getting to your Calendar app—Siri, putting it in the Dock, going through the Home Screen. As far as scheduling events, that would be best done through your iPhone rather than the Series 3. When in the Calendar app on your watch, you can toggle between the List view (for those who want to see everything they have to do that day) and the Up Next view (for those who just want to know what is up next on their schedule). You can change your view by force touching the display; this will bring up the two variations.

Reminders are just another form of notification, so what was written in the notification setting applies to reminders, as well. The best way to customize your reminder settings is through the My Watch app on your iPhone. Just know, there is no dedicated Reminders app on the Apple Watch Series 3, but that does not mean you do not have the ability to set up a reminder. You will have to utilize Siri—your assistant—to make a reminder for yourself. Tell her what you need to be reminded of and when you need to be reminded.

10. Weather app

As you would expect, the Apple Watch Series 3 also gives you information on the weather. You can see upcoming weather patterns by manually going to the app or by asking Siri. The Weather app informs you of the temperature, conditions, and chance of rain. The location(s) displayed on the Weather app on your watch will reflect those on your iPhone, so if you need to add or delete any locale, you will need to do that on the iPhone's Weather app.

PART III
Personalizing Your Apple Watch Series 3

So you have chosen the right Series 3 watch for you and now know how to operate it, but you want to make the timepiece feel like it is really yours. Throughout this book, some ways of personalizing the experiences have already been mentioned, such as deciding on the honeycomb or list view for your Home Screen and controlling what you want in your Dock. This section will get into the minutiae of the experience so that you can tailor your watch to your exact needs and desires.

1. Watch Face Design

To change the watch face design, you first need to press the digital crown to go to your watch face. Then, perform the force touch action to view the sundry designs available. You see them by swiping left or right, and most are customizable. Listed below is a selection of the best watch face designs:

<u>The Siri watch face</u> - The Siri watch face provides, perhaps, the most functional design. On a single page, the Siri watch face displays pertinent information to your day, whether it be an event you scheduled on your calendar or the ETA to your destination. This watch face

collates what you may need to know and organizes it into small bubbles that you can scroll through with the digital crown or by using the drag action. You can tap a bubble to see more information about the weather, to bring up the Maps app if you have started the direction service, etc. While not the most visually appealing watch face, the Siri face proves the most useful.

The kaleidoscope watch face - Making use of an image of your choice, the kaleidoscope watch face transforms a photograph into a pattern you would see when looking through a kaleidoscope. This watch face offers infinite possibilities as the pattern and colors will change depending on what image you select. Furthermore, if you want a unique watch face, then this would be best achieved through this watch face design as you can use photos that may be yours alone.

The photo watch face - Maybe, you are not taken by any of Apple's watch face offerings or you are simply bored of them. In this case, you can set one of your own photos as the watch face. Start the Photos app on your iPhone, select the picture you want as your watch face design, tap the Share icon and choose Create Watch Face. Here, you have the choice between the photo watch face or the kaleidoscope watch face. The change should immediately reflect on your Apple Watch's watch face.

The Activity digital face - A watch face best used when working out, the Activity watch face is linked to the Activity app, a fitness tracker. The app depicts three circles. On the outer rim, the pink circle displays how many calories you have burned; the middle circle, a green color, the number of minutes of exercise you have tracked; the innermost circle—blue—shows the amount of time you have stood up. The circles will be incomplete if you do not achieve your fitness goals for the day.

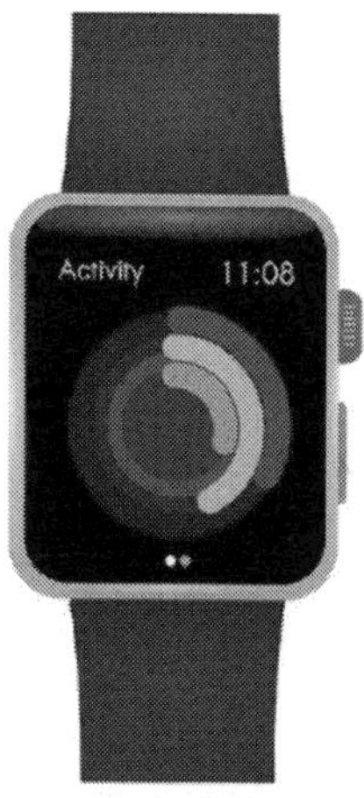

The utility watch face - The utility watch face recreates the look of a traditional watch face. It simply has the face of the usual analog watch—the time displayed with the hour, minute, second hands over a circle with the numbers 1-12 at the perimeter. As the name implies, this watch face is intended to cater to the utilitarian. This watch face does display a small version of the Activity app at the top right of the screen.

The modular watch face - Within the same vein as the utility and Siri watch faces, the modular face is all about giving you the information you need on one single page. From the weather to directions, this watch face can keep you informed with what is pertinent to you. This design will keep you from having to look at your phone. A simple design, the modular face looks like a busier digital watch face.

The motion watch face - this watch face breathes life into an otherwise static display. You can have a flower or a jellyfish on the screen, for example. You will not get much functionality out of this watch face design; nevertheless, you will have a pleasing visual without the inundation of notifications, alerts, and information on your screen every time you look at your Series 3. With this watch face design, you will get the time and date.

The astronomy watch face - Offered in Moon and Earth variants, the astronomy face allows you to interact with space. Rotating the digital crown can move time backwards or forwards engendering neighboring planets to spin and move. Pressing the digital crown returns the planets back to the current time. Another fun feature of this watch face is that tapping the Moon shows you the current lunar phase and rotating the digital crown displays future and past phases. Like the motion face, the astronomy face is not for those looking for the most utility out of their watch face. If you want to look at an uncluttered and aesthetically pleasing watch face and do not mind taking a few more steps to see your pertinent information, then this watch face is for you.

<u>The chronograph watch face</u> - The closest thing to the classic chronograph watch face, the chronograph face for the Series 3 is what its name suggests: it is a chronograph face. Those who want their Series 3 look as much like a traditional, luxury watch should consider this watch face. There are no frills or complications.

<u>The Mickey/Minnie watch face</u> - Are you a Disney fan? Or just a fan of Mickey and/or Minnie? Well, you are in luck. Apple offers a Mickey/Minnie watch face. You can choose between either of the characters by customizing the watch face. Whichever one you pick, he/she will say the time if you tap the display.

Customizing watch faces

Now, to get the watch face to display exactly the way you want it to, you need to force touch the display and then tap Customize. You will be able to tap the various 'complications' and/or pieces of information and use the digital crown to see the other options available to you. Simply press the digital crown after you are happy with the customizations you have made.

You can go about adding more complications and information to your Series 3 by going to your Apple Watch app on your iPhone. There should be a Complications section under the My Watch tab. Add a complication with the + button, remove a complication with the – button. Simple as that.

1. The Activity app

The pre-installed Activity app is Apple's fitness tracker and motivator. Essentially, you set an exercise or "move" goal, which is the amount of calories you would like to burn on a daily basis. You can set your move goal by launching the Activity app and force touching the screen. There should be an option for you to see your Weekly Summary as well as change your move goal. Increase or decrease your goal number by tapping the – and + buttons and tap Update when you have decided.

The Activity app keeps track of your movement and gives a breakdown of the exercise you have done that day. On the home screen of the app, you will see the aforementioned three circles, but if you rotate the digital crown or swipe down on the display, you will see detailed information on when and what you are doing to reach your move goal.

While the Weekly Summary may prove somewhat informative, looking at the Activity app on your iPhone gives you many more data points to get a good idea of your performance for days, weeks, months, and even years. Go on to the Activity app and tap History, which is located in the lower left corner. You will see each calendar date coupled with the recurring three vibrant Activity circles/rings. Tap one of the dates to get the full breakdown of that day, just as you can on your Apple Watch, but only for a week's worth of activity.

The Activity app, if used, makes the Apple Watch feel much more like it is yours. It gives you personal information that can give you concrete data on how you live your life. Furthermore, there are achievements to be earned, so if you need some extra motivation, you can look on your iPhone for the various awards you can win by persevering towards your fitness goals.

2. The Workout app

Closely linked to the Activity app, the Workout app is a way to track whatever exercise you want to do swimming, cycling, running, power walking, and so on. After you select the tracker that suits the type of exercise you are doing, you can see, in general, the time you have spent working out, your heart rate, and distance traveled. You can always pause a workout by pressing the digital crown and the side button simultaneously and resume with the same command. The measurements gained from a recorded Workout will transfer over to the Activity app, giving you a wholistic idea of how many calories you have burned that day.

If you want to change the metric view or the system of measurement your workouts are being recorded in, you need to go to your Apple Watch app on your iPhone. Go to the My Watch tab and tap Workout and then Workout View. You will be able to select between a Multiple Metric View (the option of having up to five metrics shown on your screen while working out) or a Single Metric View (the option of having one metric displayed on the screen at one time; you can scroll the digital crown or swipe down to see the rest of the metrics). Also, prior to starting workout, you will be setting two goals for yourself: a calorie goal and a distance goal. For those who want their calorie goal in kilometers, force touch the screen and the option will pop up. The same can be done for your distance goal, but you will be choosing between yards/ miles and meters/kilometers.

3. Make sure to enjoy Apple Music

This especially applies to those who have the Series 3 Cellular and bought a plan with a provider. Since you have the data, you can stream music for your daily life or workouts without needing to bring your phone along. Also, you need to use your monthly data anyways, so using it on streaming could be a good way to maximize your coverage.

But those with the GPS-only version of the Series 3 can still listen to music on the go, but they will need to bring their iPhone along. However, you can download your music to your Apple Watch so that you do not need cellular connectivity to listen to music. You will not have virtually limitless variety, but there is no extra charge involved. Depending on how much music you want to have on your watch, you might have to keep a watchful eye on your storage, though.

4. Download third-party apps

While Apple provides most of the basic apps you will need, it does not hurt to supplement your catalogue with third-party apps that can add a great deal of functionality to your Apple Watch.

i. *Calcbot*

Perhaps, to many people's understandable surprise, the Apple Watch does not come with a calculator app. Having the Calcbot app—just a basic calculator—makes paying exact tips much more convenient, for example. You will not need to take out your phone to make any calculation you might have to do in your daily life. The app is also free, which is always a plus.

ii. *Evernote*

Another surprising omission from Apple's stock apps, a note taking tool did not make the cut for the Apple Watch Series 3. Nevertheless, you can download Evernote for free so that you can take notes on the go. Notes are recorded through dictation.

iii. *iTranslate*

For those times when you are off adventuring in a country where English is not widely spoken or learned, the iTranslate app translates your sentences into the native tongue of the country you are visiting. Just dictate to the app and it will immediately output a translation for you. Gone are those awkward moments of gesturing and speaking slowly.

iv. Sleep++

With the prevalence of mattress commercials these days, proper sleep seems to be a great concern for most these days. Sleep++ monitors your sleep and gives you information on what you need to do to improve your nightly rest. This app could engender the healthy change you might need in your life.

v. Uber

Uber is premier ridesharing app, and you can get it on your Apple Watch Series 3. You will get all the information you would normally get through the phone version of the app (Driver ETA, car model, etc.).

5. Remove the apps you do not want, even the stock ones

Perhaps at one point in your life, you had an interest in the stock market, but now it does not bring you the enjoyment it once did. Your Apple Watch came with the Stocks app pre-installed, and you would rather use your storage for other apps. Apple has given users full authority on what apps they have on their watch, including the apps Apple designed for the watch. If you do not want it, you can delete it. Of course, you invariably have the option to download the Apple apps for free if you ever want to in the future.

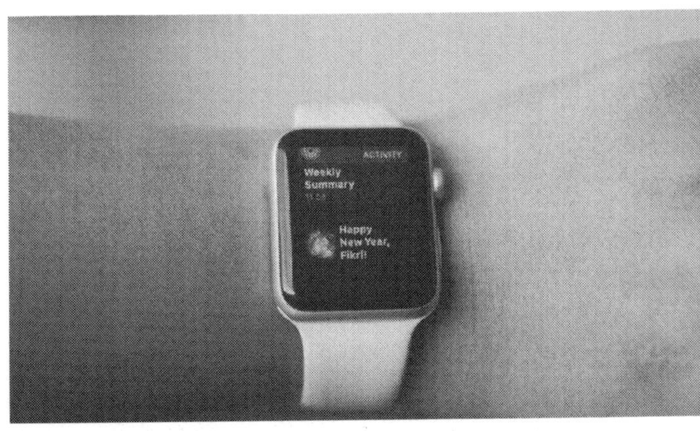

PART IV
Tips & Tricks

For lefties: If you are a left-handed person, you can change the watch orientation so the device suits you best. Simply go to the Apple Watch app on your iPhone and go to the General tab. Once there, click Watch Orientation.

Create multiple watch faces that you have customized: Creating multiple watch faces may not sound like something you want to do—you like a particular watch face and you are opposed to changing it. Sure, that could be the case, but having multiple watch faces allows you to quickly switch to a different design that best suits what you are doing. When you are exercising, you might want to select the Activity watch face with particular Complications. Later, you might be going to an upscale restaurant, so you want to go with the chronograph watch face. Creating multiple watch faces that you have customized to work with your tastes eliminates repeated alterations and time-wasting.

Forcing your Apple Watch to restart: Once in a while, devices tend to act up, suddenly slowing down or just refusing to function normally. Perhaps, your watch has frozen. In these cases, you can force restart your watch by pressing and holding the digital crown and side button simultaneously for ~10 seconds. You can cease holding when the Apple logo appears on the screen. Let it be known, though, force restarting your Apple Watch should be done as a last resort, per Apple. You should try to wait it out, instead. If nothing serious is wrong with the device, it should recover its optimal functionality soon enough.

Switching on power reserve: Perhaps, you are quickly running out of battery and you have left your phone at home. Turning on the power reserve mode on your Series 3 prolongs battery life so you will not have to worry about getting stranded somewhere without a functioning mobile device. This mode shuts off everything but your Series 3's ability to tell time. Supposedly, turning on power reserve mode extends battery life up to 72 hours. Thus, before your Series 3 reaches a critical battery state, you can turn on this mode so that when you need the juice to call someone later, your watch will have the requisite battery life to function. When your battery reaches a low percentage, your Apple Watch will automatically switch on power reserve; however, if you want to manually activate it, you need to go to the Control Center (swipe up from the watch face screen) and tap your battery reading. The option to turn on power reserve will be on that page.

Crafting your stock responses on Messages: For those times when you want to text something you often do—a "where are you?" or "Love you, X"—you can set up your personal stock responses to send through Messages. Apple does provide a few pre-written messages, but if to someone you often text, such as your significant other, you can add a little personal flair to your pre-written responses. You can go about writing these stock responses on the Apple Watch app on your iPhone. Once the app has started, you need to go to the Messages setting and then tap Default Replies to craft your own stock responses.

Muting alerts with your palm: Apple provides an ingenious way to mute your alerts and notifications when you rest your palm over you Series 3. This means you do not have to go through the inconvenience of turning mute mode on and off. To activate this gesture, go to the My Watch app on your iPhone and tap Sounds & Haptics. Turn on the Cover to Mute. You will need to cover your Apple Watch for three seconds for it to register the mute command. You will know that the watch has been muted when it vibrates.

Taking photos with the Series 3: Lacking a camera to take photos, the Apple Watch Series 3 oddly comes with the Camera app pre-installed. This is for good reason, however. The Apple Watch Series 3 becomes a remote shutter trigger for your iPhone's camera. You simply need to open the Camera app on your Apple Watch and the same app will start on your paired iPhone. This way you can operate the camera while still being in the photo. So on those family trips when you want everyone to be present in the photo, the Apple Watch provides a solution.

Taking a screenshot: If, for whatever reason, you want to take a screenshot of what is currently on your Apple Watch display, you can press the digital crown and the side button simultaneously. The screenshot will be sent to your saved photographs.

Pinging your iPhone: Lost your iPhone? It happens to the best of us. But the Series 3 allows you to easily locate your iPhone by activating the Ping command from the watch's Control Center. Tap the icon with a phone and vibrations and your phone will vibrate and make a pinging noise. But, perhaps the ping is not enough. In this case, press the same icon, thus starting the LED flash on your phone and giving you a visual cue as to where your iPhone is.

Blocking water out from your Series 3: If you want to go for a swim or simply take a shower with your watch on, you can go to the Control Center and tap the icon with the water droplet on it. This will lock your watch casing, sealing it from exposure to water. This will also clear out the water from your Series 3's device. So in the case that water has gotten into the speaker, for example, tapping the water droplet will clear out any of that water blockage.

Setting your Series 3 a few minutes ahead: For those who want to make sure they are early rather than late to whatever they have scheduled, you can set your Apple Watch a few minutes ahead of the actual time so that you can remain on top of everything. To change the time on your Apple Watch, go to the Settings app, tap Time, and then just decide how much time you would like to add to the actual time. Remember: your notification, reminders, events, etc. will come in at that the actual time, not your personal time.

Unlocking your Apple computer(s) with the Apple Watch: If you own any Apple computer, the Apple Watch can be used to unlock your Mac without having to type in your password. First, you need to make sure both devices are on the same iCloud account. To set up the Series 3's unlock function, you need to go to System Preferences on your computer and then click on the General tab in Security & Privacy.

Set up Apple Pay: A veritably convenient app, Apple Pay gives you the liberty to go around without needing your credit and/or debit cards. Just go to the app and input your card information and you will be able to use the app to pay bills with your watch.

Checking your data usage: Maybe you are a workout fiend and have been going out on long runs every day of the month. You have been streaming music the whole time, and are worried about how much data you have been using. Oddly enough, you cannot check your data usage on the Apple Watch Series 3, so you will have to check it on your iPhone. To view your data usage, go to the My Watch app on your iPhone and then go to Mobile Data (it might show up as Cellular). Not only will you be able to see how much data you have used for the month, you will get a breakdown of how much data each of your apps are using. You can use these figures as a reference point for how you want to go about deploying your watch in the future.

Sending your location: If you are having trouble explaining your location to your friend, you can just share your location with your contacts. Using the Messages app, find the person you want to send your location information to and force touch the display. Three options will pop up: Reply; Details: and Send Location. Obviously, you need to tap Send Location and your current location, per GPS and GLONASS, will be immediately sent to that contact.

Enlarging text: If your sight is not the best, you have the option of increasing the text size in order for you to see the text on your Series 3 without having to squint. You need to go to the Settings app on your watch, tap General, and tap the Brightness & Text Size button. At this screen, select Text Size and rotate your digital crown to achieve the exact text size you desire.

Tinker with your Apple Watch: The last tip is to simply play around with your Series 3 to see what you can get out of the different apps you already have on your watch or have downloaded. Tap around, force touch the display, swipe in all directions—just tinker with your watch. It does not hurt to know how to navigate your watch in the way that is most efficient for you. And who knows, you might discover some secret functions that will exponentially improve your efficacy.

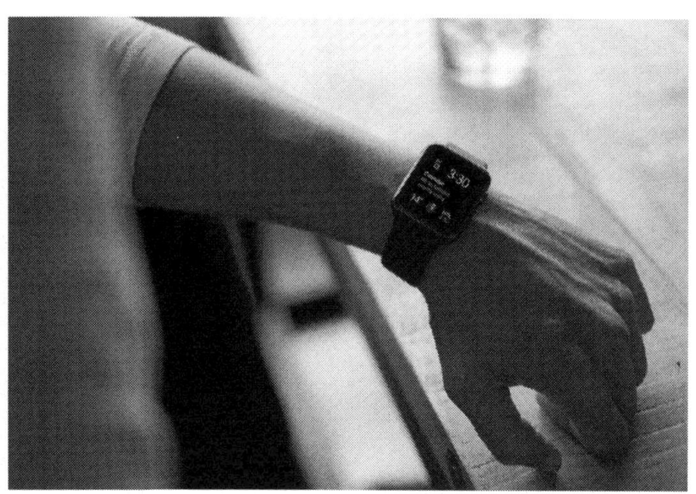

Conclusion

The possibilities to customize and personalize your Apple Watch Series 3 can prove daunting at times, but this guide has hopefully provided you with a comprehensive overview of everything you need to know about purchasing and using your timepiece. More than a traditional watch, where the functions and features are limited, the Apple Watch truly allows you to have an experience of your own that goes beyond the appearance and machinery of the watch.

In part I, this book covered all the available options for customizing the look of your Series 3. As with purchasing anything, it is always best to have researched what exactly goes into the product you desire. The jargon used to describe technological products especially sounds complicated and serves as good ad copy, however it is necessary to know what the tech does for you as the user. Perhaps, this book has informed you of the tech involved in the Apple Watch, while also supplying an exhaustive list of the cosmetic options available to you.

In part II, this book intended to furnish you with an in-depth tutorial on how to operate the Apple Watch Series 3. Navigating the watch can be difficult initially, but this book has all the information you need to figure out the basic operations and main apps of the watch. As you continue to use the watch, surely you will grow more and more comfortable with it; operating it will probably become second nature to you. Nevertheless, as you awkwardly fumble around with it in the early stages, you can always refer back to part II to get concise guidance on what you need to do to get your Apple Watch functioning the way you want it to.

In part III, this book went over one of the crowning features of the Apple Watch Series 3: the capacity to make the watch completely your own. Whether it be customizing your watch face design so that it works best for your life or setting your personal fitness goals, the Series 3 is crafted to be wholly yours. It seems injudicious to not personalize your watch so that it does exactly what you need/want it to do—that appears to be the whole point of a smartwatch! Ideally, this book encourages you to tinker around with your settings until you get the watch exactly how you want it.

In part IV, this book provided an exhaustive list of tips and tricks in using your Apple Watch Series 3. Following some of them will really give you the opportunity to maximize your usage of the watch. You will be patting yourself on the back when you lose your iPhone and can find it with the Ping command on your Apple Watch. Hopefully, you will not have misplaced both.

Ultimately, this book should have provided you with all the information you need to get the most out of your Apple Watch Series 3. No stone has been left unturned in the making and writing of this book.

Made in the USA
San Bernardino, CA
27 August 2018